Flower Gardens

by Melvin and Gilda Berger

SCHOLASTIC INC.

ISBN 978-0-545-47658-4

Copyright © 2013 by Melvin & Gilda Berger

All rights reserved. Published by Scholastic Inc. SCHOLASTIC and associated logos are trademarks and/or registered trademarks of Scholastic Inc.

12 11 10 9 8 7 6 5   15 16 17 18/0

Printed in the U.S.A.   40
First printing, March 2013

Photo Credits: Photo Research: Alan Gottlieb

Cover: © Frank Lukasseck/Getty Images; Back cover: © Thinkstock; Title page: © iStockphoto/Thinkstock; page 3: © Ariel Skelley/Corbis/Media Bakery; page 4: © Imagemore Co., Ltd./Corbis; page 5: © Unlisted Images/Corbis; page 6: © Thinkstock; page 7: © Adam Jones/Getty Images; page 8: © National Geographic/SuperStock; page 9: © Dr. John Brackenbury/Photo Researchers, Inc.; page 10: © iStockphoto/Thinkstock; page 11: © Thinkstock; page 12: © Shutterstock, Inc.; page 13: © Joel Douillet/Alamy; page 14: © Thinkstock; page 15: © Adam Jones/Visuals Unlimited/Getty Images; page 16: © Glow Image

Flowers grow in flower gardens.

Which flowers are tallest?

Some gardens have a mix of flowers.

Some have only one kind of flower.

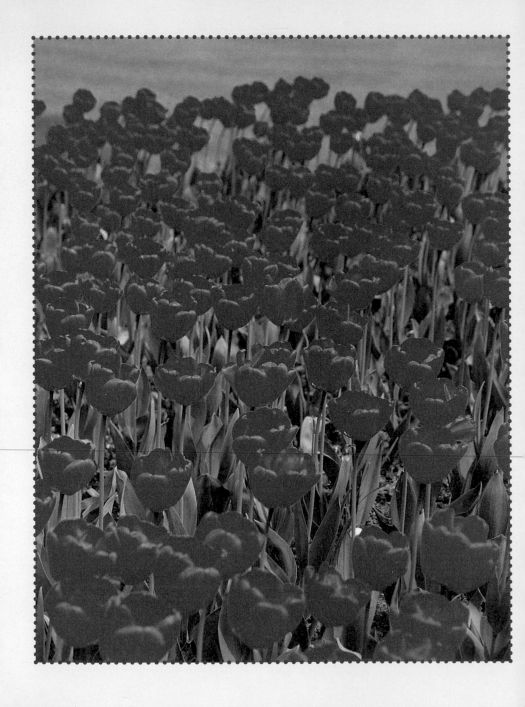

Tulips grow in spring.

How many colors do you see?

Tulips come in many colors.

Snapdragons grow in summer.

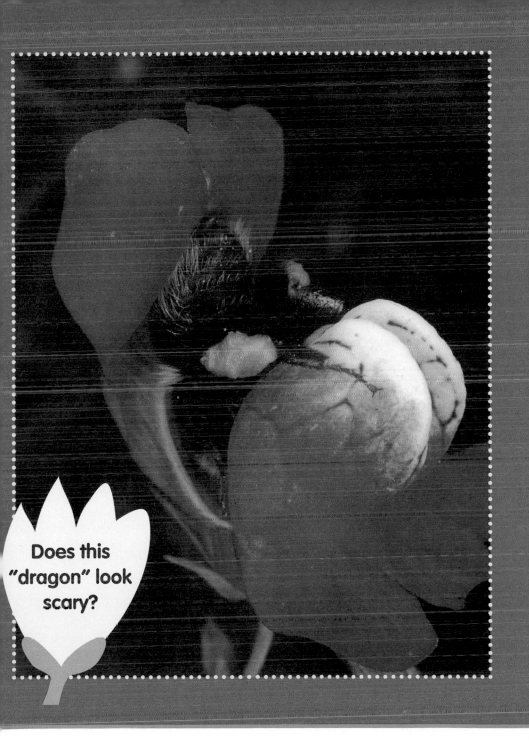

Does this "dragon" look scary?

Each flower looks like a dragon's head.

Asters grow in fall.

Can you find the stems and leaves?

Each flower has many petals.

Marigolds live for only one year.

Where are the marigolds in this garden?

Flowers that live for only one year are called annuals.

Daylilies come back year after year.

Where are the daylilies in this garden?

Flowers that come back year after year are called perennials.

Ask Yourself

1. What grows in flower gardens?
2. Do tulips grow in spring or fall?
3. When do asters grow?
4. How long do marigolds live?
5. Are daylilies annuals or perennials?

You can find the answers in this book.